Trembling
of the
City

Hagit Grossman

Trembling of the City

translated from Hebrew by
Benjamin Balint

Shearsman Books

First published in the United Kingdom in 2016 by
Shearsman Books
50 Westons Hill Drive
Emersons Green
BRISTOL
BS16 7DF

Shearsman Books Ltd Registered Office
30–31 St. James Place, Mangotsfield, Bristol BS16 9JB
(this address not for correspondence)

www.shearsman.com

ISBN 978-1-84861-477-2

ACKNOWLEDGEMENTS
Trembling of the City was first published in Hebrew in 2014
by Keshev Publishers, Tel Aviv.

CONTENTS

The Hall of Magic

Evolution

I was once a paleolithic painter, a sensual hunter
plundering the earth, living from hand to mouth,
I painted at the cave's corner, concerned only with the day's concerns.
Faithful to nature, I rendered beauty straight and pure
Sketching motion in lightning strokes,
I saw nuanced shades finer than fine.
I did not know of shadows
Believed neither in gods nor in the world to come.
I lived in an age of actions.
Then I fragmented and fissured the world into
reality and beyond
the visible and the hidden
the mortal and the soul.

Defective Evolution

I sense evolution is defective
no guitar sprouted forth from me where it should,
my parents immigrated to the wrong country,
and Paris is too far away.

I sense evolution is defective
the fingers are too lazy to tell the gospel,
Romance drowned herself in the stream,
and the brackish waters demanded their due after her demise.

I sense evolution is defective in those volumes of poetry:
words are dragged by their hair into the green reeds
and splayed across the stream,
their blind sputtering verses afloat,
adrift beside corpses of rock'n'roll,
intellectuals, poets and all the others
who whored themselves
to adapt to the atmosphere.

I sense evolution is defective
on the seam that separates laptop and typewriter,
My libido never awakens to the glows of a screen
but paper arouses me.

I sense evolution is defective
once I declaimed poetry on stage with an orchestra
once I soared with the music.
Afterward I couldn't utter a single loveless word
Afterward I knew I'd touched the loveliest thing I'd ever know
and ever since I sense evolution is defective.

Trembling
of the
City

My Tormentlove

Forgive me if I fall on your shoulder
Inside the wind is too strong
I ought to scream now and become sick, it is a sickness of war
The wind erupts red from my hair which hid all winter
Between the books
And a madman who was not afraid to love a woman
Made me feel special
Came to wish me good night
And to make me a cup of tea.
Behind the wall, a woman screamed on the staircase.
Bathed in sweat, I lay beside him
A slave to the love of strangers,
My mouth torn upwards, my arms sent into the air
The tea spilled, puddled on the tablecloth.
I'll never forget him, that time when all the paintings were in purple
But one day the door swung open and I saw he had aged.
He laid himself out in my room, I asked him to stay,
And I dressed in his clothes.

You

1

I remember how Jerusalem
made wolf's teeth grow in my mouth
and I would lurk for you in the streets.
If you had come across me —
that coldness around the pupil,
that strangeness —
I would have gashed you with my teeth
and howled to God:
Thank you, thank you.
Maybe you will never know
how you were Death to me
and the more I chose you the more there lived within me
the illusion. And the body, that was made
for the love of your flesh, sprouted flesh
and my belly gushed forth pure love.
I hide in my room
and the blood that had made dreams quake
turns now to terror
casts off the essentials of love.
This terror has scissors that cut breath,
that crush air into a blinding dust
and the river of splendor flows through life
washing away remorse as it courses down
and whenever I hear children singing
the wounds of your memories are forgotten, clarified away like fools.
Even through the heart of illusion flows the river of life
and the poem is the holding-point inside it.

2

You who were my Death
climb now from the cellar and hover in the gloom
my soul was in your hands
like a gypsy girl on her wedding day
my dress is a flawless white
your body, hurtful, is fixed in my flesh.
All the way from you to me
I heard footsteps behind me
I turned to find no one there
the footsteps were my own.
I wanted to be wonderful for you
but only the attraction and the lies were real.
All the way from you to me, my voice kept me alive,
it enveloped me in the poem's skin
buried in my heart a subtle clear Spring.
Your mouth's vapor in mine
a grey river blowing
on all that was in me before you
and all the waters know it is me.

Jerusalem in South Tel Aviv

Tonight the last wall between us crumbled
and your secret fell into me.
Tonight I knew that always, always.
In the darkness
everything you don't say is whispered:
Yeho-Natan, God has given me your love
that I will know a word which chases fear away
and in this word is Jerusalem.

Distance

The distance from you was as real as glass shards scraped over flesh
If blood spurts from me, you will play the fool and make me laugh
You don't fear me, it would be terrible to leave you
The city's darkness whispers the distance from your body
I face the letters naked
Like when I lay on the bed crying
and you wiped down my wet body with a damp cloth
and I thought I might die in a moment if you did not leave.
And your voice roped around my neck
and I went to the shower and the rope is dragged behind me.
I wanted to paint the wall yellow and you waited for me on the bed
I wished that you would disappear, that I could be someone else
and you painted the walls purple
the bedroom blue
and the girl's room pink
and on her wall we discovered the name you gave her
engraved in timeworn letters,
and you knew you had powers of sorcery
and I knew it too.

Trembling of the City

The interior city trembled
and I sensed a need to feel truly sorry and beg forgiveness
to know that the city would never be the same
because the trust and quiet in the dark alleys of its heart had been disturbed.
In the middle of the living-room we let outside observers get involved,
and come in and sit on the red sofa.
And they have that realistic look of math teachers
with their cold glances and high salaries
and we are locked into poetry books
we are a citadel whose walls have fallen
because I let anger burst through and curse what was.
And those observers with the cold glances
said they came with love
and admitted that we had entrusted them with a great power
capable of razing sacred cities.
And you no longer gazed into my eyes, you became distant,
You turned off the light and went to sleep,
Leaving me beside you in the dark.
I whispered your name, but you gave no reply
I wanted to feel sorry and beg forgiveness
and touched your warm body, and you did not touch me back.

Bicycle

The bond tightened, like the chain of a bicycle straining uphill
toward realization of an artful thought.
Or pulling downhill, toward silence.
On the plain, we found fairy dust on the pillowed meadows.
On the plain, we would remember our love
and the bond kept trundling the bike through the houred lanes
without lull or rest.
At night we became black fish.
The bike was left on the shore
Together we plumbed the depths
And spoke there of that which only we shall know.

*

We loved to abuse our love,
To tug it from side to side, to shake it, to turn our backs,
To watch it suffer from neglect, from fury, from muteness,
silenced to its choked heart.
We liked to torment our love,
To test how long it could hold its breath underwater.
Four hands gripped around its throat,
We would wait for it to cough and sputter back to life,
Its eyes bloodshot with loneliness
Until laughter burst from its brokenness and we could be together again.
Turning away from its blood streaming beneath the bed
From everything it wanted to say.

Love Poem for a Cook from Florentine Street

I won't corner you into small spaces
I'll pull up a sofa wherever you want to rest your head
I now know how
When everyone else is out celebrating
You hide among the pots.

When everyone goes out into the streets
You enclose yourself in a narrow room
They are gorged, and you haven't rested since morning
Though there is a war on, the restaurant is full.

Rooftop

One night I'll go up to the roof
The heavens will be blued like indigo
A wind will whirl past. The towers will gleam like dogs
With phosphorescent poison. The silence will annihilate the stars
I'll lie down on the lumpy filthy couch
And I'll be filled with the hushed wind and I won't care
That there is no access to the roof,
Because the shitty landlord rented it to someone
And blocked it to anyone else
I'll write a poem to that faceless landlord
I'll roast him and feed him to the dogs.
Four years now I've been boxed in,
Fantasizing about a wider balcony
About breezes, about open spaces,
While above my head the roof dwells
Coupled to the clouds, to the heavens, to God.
But the money-men have locked the door.

At the Corner of the Margins

In the south of the city, in a neighborhood of decaying tenements
Is a girl on a desolate bench
Wearing a tight dress, her legs bare
Crossed, chafing against her dream
That a man will appear, reach out, and lift her out of the trash.
The scent of her body is sweet, like a promise kept,
A body so beautifully flawed, tall and imperfect
Like a fruit that has had its nectar sipped
And still, at the bottom is an endless well.
The flawed body — the neglected, the betrayed, the accursed,
The despised, the only one — which arouses a dream of another body,
That no man will love
As she never quite managed to say:
"You are beautiful, body, thank you for your shell."
In the sidewalk gutter is a young man
His face blackened and his forehead wounded red.
Facing the stoplights, a steaming sated cold
That will not comprehend an empty stomach.

Shrieks

How many shrieks are in my head
A man is a lunatic asylum
You could summon a whole minyan to say kaddish.
How many deaths are in my head
But not a shekel for rent or bread.
Poets have been banished from large cities
Unless they are wealthy heirs or beggars
Who speak the truth
In which case no one listens to them anyway.
In general they get fired from their jobs
Or quit on principle.

In the Market Square

In the market square, in the shade of a Harley-Davidson,
Sits Jesus smoking a cigarette,
Forgetting his days in the lunatic asylum.
Gnawing at large rolls made from white flour,
Gulping lemon juice straight from the fruit.
What would happen if we approached him with a cross?
We would chase him between the bread stalls,
Smear his blood on a baguette.
Skeptics crowd round his red cloak.
His hairy chest exposed to the wind.
He inscribes twenty new commandments
On white cardboard.
His face smeared on the pavement
On a billboard that shouts: Compassion!
He sits there with an avocado
And red Marlboros.
What shall we do to the new Jesus?
How shall we eat him?
What shall we do with his flesh?
What shall we do to this man who sits in the market square
Like a bear with a biblical license
magnetizing all the poor wretches.
A man who found power
Or power that found a lunatic
Wants to carve out a new religion
In the heart of the city.

Poem for an Addict

A poem for an addict who infuriates me
I didn't give her a coin because once
She had a full and beautiful face
And now the drugs have eroded her cheeks
And she looks like a corpse begging for spare coins
And I gave two to Andre the drunk and none to her
And I told Andre I'd write a poem about him
And Andre was glad and stood next to me
On the street corner and wandered around
And didn't want to leave
And then she came
With something that had once been a smile
And she puckered up and tried to lift her cheeks
And I told her that I'd given everything
To Andre
And she smiled with embarrassment and walked away
And I dragged her home on my back
And couldn't fall asleep
Because of her hellish body, still smoldering
And the regret that I hadn't given her a shekel
Or fifty. All in all
Just a bill in my purse
All in all just a ticket
To something connected to life.

The Dream of a Million

The dream of a million crouched on her heart
Heavy and hemmed in like an air-conditioned apartment
A window with a full moon. A silent hour.
She sits in the café and talks
About what would be when she started to work.
"Then I'll have money," she says
And drags on a Vogue cigarette.
Her bleached hair hangs tired
But her wrinkled face does not surrender
Does not know how to dangle dreams
On any other threads.

Cheese Monger

At the age of fifty-five she worked in a cheese shop
From dawn to dusk
For twenty-three shekels an hour.
Thorny rosebushes blossomed on her transparent cheeks
Beneath the chilling look of a woman
Whose face had shed its leaves of beauty
Who never received a kind word
Whose tears halted in her eyes and refused to ease the burden
She had the look of one who had given up.
Young women would whisper that she had a mean face
They didn't grasp the reason she kept to herself
Laboring to sustain a body that requires nourishment
Though the soul within has gone silent.
Her husband was a hard man, refused her kisses
Removed her arms from around him and did not whisper love .
After he left she found this job
In the cheese shop. In the back yard a black dog barks.
Every morning she offers him cheese and milk
And whispers to him:
My love, my love.

Romance

To Beck

I offer you the rusty pan
I'm eating from. I place it on the floor
And trust in good karma that you will come close
And in the beauty of a hand sent down
To give you slices of spiced meat.
Your tongue laps the pan and your large eyes
Shine lovingly brown.
A cunning February wind,
Its sharpness leading me after you
Between the tables of the drunks of King George Street
A woman with a nose-piercing crouches down to you
Strokes your black back.
You keep pulling me into the stripes of sun and shade.
Afterwards, shut in the back yard, you growl and howl at my window.
I throw you a piece of bloody liver,
You chew it and calm down.

Poem for a Filipino Baby

On karaoke nights no one puts you to sleep.
You rub your eyes, and they sing in English,
If you can't beat 'em, boy, join 'em
Sing, boy — it's your fate,
A crowded one-room flat with three women and one man,
A small playpen in the corner and a future shining floors.
Sing, boy — it's New Year's Eve and the tall man is singing about angels,
You won't sleep tonight, boy, in your blue pajamas,
Mommy embraces you and sings,
She'll never again leave you in the dark room,
Sing, boy — they're shouting and laughing,
It's the new year and the neighbors will call the cops soon
They'll take you from here, so sing now — don't be afraid.

*

I'll be strong now
Like a gay Filipino who lives in a one-room flat
With three women and a baby, I'll be strong like him
I'll put on dark glasses, a clean purple shirt,
Like him I'll raise a little black dog,
I'll open the door to the balcony and let her
Out to bark at passing cars.
Bark out your crowded confinement,
Your smallness and blackness and furriness,
In a roomful of bunk beds and the cries of a baby thirsty
For his mother's voice.
Bark, dog, to a world made indifferent by car engines and horns.
Howl like that big dog enclosed for five years now
In the back yard, cry for the caress of the cheese-monger,
For her soft strokes on his whitening forehead
Curled up all night in its kennel
Trying to escape the lashing cold.

On the Sidewalk

He was crumpled on the sidewalk
Like a mangled wallet full of foreign coins
Which no one would pocket.
I was startled by his legs, bound by death,
By his blood, poisoned with the fire of forgetting,
By his eyes, marked by a rusty needle,
And I dared not approach to lift him from the pavement
To restore him to the land of the living.
His fall had cast darkness over the street
But my hands fell short
And my legs sought the nearest bus stop.
When I tried to gather the last signs of breath from his body
My legs took me far away
To the windows of my home, shuttered
Against the winds that had battered his body.

The Villain

The villain sits in the violet car and smokes a cigarette
His eyebrows sharpened, and his car jammed in traffic
He notices a woman smiling at him and fails to remember
That he once fucked up her life
With his deceptive theories and his decadence.
His cock passed from hand to hand and he lived in darkness
Forgetting where the hand came from and where the responsibility lay.
That woman from the street – her man was pure:
There was something real between them.
For the villain he was just a rag to whom he spoon-fed
Deceptive theories about the good life in the darkness,
To wake up in unkempt beds in strange streets,
To take drugs and record songs for the radio
Meaningless songs, songs in gibberish.
The scoundrel worked hard extorting money from innocent guys
Like that man who offered his life to the woman from the street
And one victim-strewn night she betrayed him with the villain,
He defiled her young body with his pale weak seed.
And today she walks in the street and remembers
And he sits stuck in his car and forgets
Smoking and looking at her with eyes that strain to shed light.

On Friendship

If a friend calls out to you late at night from beneath your window
Never send him on his way. And if you've sent him away and still
Insist on rigid rules, regain your composure after a moment
And run to the window and shout his name: "Come, Merhav!
Come back! I've got some corn cooking! Come eat something."
And he'll placidly retrace his steps and gladly accept
The key you toss down from your window
Will come upstairs to the first floor and will be impressed
By the large pictures on the walls.
He'll sit and wait for you to slip into a clean shirt and you'll put on
The movie in the kid's room and your baby daughter
Will rush to the kitchen and come back with a red pepper for him.
He'll decline the warm corn and say he's already had dinner.
In the meantime your husband will chat with him about Tai Chi
And pour him a glass of cold sweet pineapple juice.
You'll return to the living room
And go out to the balcony and light a cigarette and sip
A cold beer. You don't yet realize
That this is a sublime moment in your life,
One of the most sublime you'll ever know.

Love

The toilet clogged up like the collective heart unable
To listen to the secret of Brigitte Bardot,
Whose beauty was not in her body but in her heart. I'm sure
That Chuck Alberts would eat vegetable soup with her just because
She loves animals almost as much as he does.
Both have very warm hearts
Where a green giant sits
Afraid of overheating
And bursting from his yearning
For a world that would advance and become
A better place. Brigitte Bardot's dress
Would be made of natural materials and Chuck
Would slip it off only if she consents.
Some say that work is the most important thing
But Chuck knows that life is the most important thing.
That this war is a substitute for sex
That if only we knew how to nurture the skills
Of love, Brigitte Bardot would become head of the UN
And Chuck Alberts would become the sun that illuminates the dark.

The Hall of Magic

The Hall of Magic

Rosa Silber rose to the heights on ladders
From hidden passages to flashlight beams
Rosa climbed to where the hall of sorcerers became
A hall of ghosts, until her strings came loose
She wanders the streets in search of those who hold the strings
Reflected in display windows and skyrockets on nervous breakdown wings
A repressed fire burns her heart
Monologues at the corners of her mouth are stretched on the end-bed
Rosa waves a silvery wand and dances at the street corner
Where there are no sins except forgetting
She managed to disappear before the Angel of Acceptance appeared
Her youth stripped from her skin
Her soul also went walking in a familiar land
That until now had been her place of exile
Its houses no longer gilded, nor maddened
But all is quite grey now in the hall of magic.

Letter to a Poet who Stopped Writing

You wrote to him that you no longer write poetry
He cannot change anything except
to quote Qohelet for you
to tell you to observe the passage of time
and to surrender. Do not yearn for days past.
But you always glance back
what remains there shimmers
and still captivates your eyes.
You want to gather in that freedom
and bring it to the nest,
Sparkling necklaces of lifeless moments
bracelets encrusted with illusory freedom
before you met, when loneliness was chains.
It is so easy to flee when you are not free.
Not to write poetry.
Not to think. Not to speak.
You always wanted someone to come into the room.
The one who caused you to write. To crave.

How to Come at Things

How to come at things if not from the back.
In the light of day
a black cat paces on the sixth-floor ledge.
Hamlet in fur. A black skull.
A dry-throated woman, enslaved to her home,
throws an empty bucket at its back;
its paws are wet, it does not fall.
In the light of the sixth day
someone has to do it.
Coffee, cigarette, there's no time.
A woman enslaved to her home,
How to come at things if not from behind,
by hiding to exhale, dry-mouthed vaporing, a thirst for poetry.
Every poet relies on his poetry as if it were another space in a cell.
Perhaps one should come at things from the bowels,
and from there climb up to the eyes and ask:
"Which things exactly?"

Poetry

Sometimes Poetry's rooms are closed and I knock at the door.
I stand outside Poetry and knock and knock:
"Let me in, I want in."
It's Wednesday afternoon and I'm outside Poetry's gates,
Waiting for my furious mother to give me back a key to her home.
Bit by bit, this greyness trims the green branches of hope.
The wolves of wrath howl:
"Open for us, open up; come spirit, and I'll converse with you,
Come, spirit, and I'll sing."

I spread open my heart to gather up words that I wrote to her
from between her thighs.

After she stayed silent and refused to let me into her home,
The phone rang and no one answered.
The trees in the street stood silvery bare,
Entangled, expectant.
Someone threatened to burn all the books.
To transcribe words into flickering illusions.
The dogs were left trapped in their kennels.
Cannons thundered in vain.
Libraries stood in the shame of yellowing pages.
Only electric current flowed through black cables
Flooded in horrible loneliness.

After she left me outside her gates, I feared for her well-being.
I thought she might be at home, dying, and I wanted to stand at her bedside.
I knew she had been betrayed by malignant electronics
And her spirit had expired from negligence.

After I was left outside her home
I enclosed myself in the empty studio and photographed my eye
With a tiny video camera.
Reflected in my eye, strange and unsightly.

The girls danced and sang in the other room.
She always let them in,
She loves them, and they speak of her naturally.

After she left me outside her gates,
I beat against her door until my wits drained away.
I consumed rich Brazil nuts and sugar-glazed pineapple,
Tensed my muscles for the next blow on her door.
I already thought of restraining my body, of not looking for her.
To be nothing more than famished flesh,
To live without remembering, to walk without watching,
To be a listening but unhearing body,
Scattered on the winds of amusement.
Not to wait until she calls my name.
Yet every day I beat against her door
And I taught others the way to her,
Revealing to them her secret.
I disclosed all the words that were written describing her essence.

And maybe she's just a whore, blinding them,
Extorting delicate minds to trust in Eternity.
She will clasp tight homeless paupers,
She will blow the drug of Eternity into their gasping lungs.
And all night they will make love to her
And with rivulets of ink will blow in her hair.
They will whisper her beauty in rented rooms,
Will speak to the dwellers of the walls,
To the dawning sun,
To the piece of bread they purchase with their last ounce of blood.
She doesn't desire the others,
Just those who yearn enough to turn their backs on the world,
To let her pass through their bones,
To lend her their bodies,
So that out of them she can make
Poetry.

Reading

I am reading poetry. My body becomes one with the empty hall
Above the packed hall. My voice rides the elevator, ascends.
I press the buttons of the heavens and all the circuits
Whirl into action and invite the angels
The elevator rises into the hemorrhaging heavens
Fingers grasp the microphone but feel nothing
Blood rushes to the faces of the women poets in the first row
They send me the cackling of witches and black light
Plunges into in me like a knife. But on the other side
Sits Anat Levin haloed in white light
And she adorns me with her good soul
And I'm already on the eighth floor.
The strings of Ophir's guitar hoist the good psychiatrist
Toward the ceiling and a spray of ricocheting bullets.
I dash down a carpet of red shadows
And billions of dollars plunge with me into the firmament
And I am there and my whole body goes up in smoke.
The music ceases, the poem ends, the microphone returns to its place
and I step down from the stage.

To Anat

Even if you will not become a mother, know that you have known love
Greater than any ever known.
You envelop him at night. He is your son.
He loves you as only a poet can
He will never leave your bed
For him you are singular.
Even if you don't become a mother, know that you have known love.
Your face imprinted with a burning calm
Because you wanted to be his son's mother
You caress his head, you recite his poems
And his image is reflected in your kindly eyes.
Only a poet would wish to love so deeply
Only a great soul like yours cries out at night to give.
Don't cry, dear sister,
Even if you don't become a mother, know that you have known love.
Your body embraces his, he breathes your words,
You are his mother and he is your father. Your child. Your brother.
You are shielded from the night
Don't wait until dawn. See that love has approached your bed
Where a loyal man lies in a room encased in memories
And a single will to pass the barren time
And there is no barrenness except in loneliness
And you are not alone.
One day he will call your name
And your home will brim over with the laughter of children.
Your tarrying child will open the door and run into your arms.

The Boy with the Blue Hat

The boy with the blue hat
Would kick and write with infinitely strong thighs
Freedom gripping his neck. He would hallucinate
Poems and toss words into the street
That no one had heard and no one understood.
What a winter it was
For the boy in the blue hat
Who made himself disappear behind
The big belly and wore a maternity
Dress and would complain about
The loss of those strong thighs.
Each morning added a wailing complaint
And the blue hat was no more.
Just then people began listening
To the boy in the blue hat
And themselves putting on
Blue hats
And there was one old man, wise and tall,
Who sang the praises of the boy in
The blue hat who went and withdrew
Into the body of the woman
Who had knitted it.

The Speed of Everything

The speed of everything drives through the flesh.
What was she if not a tool of transmission?
And she beat the drums of life
so as not to forget
she sought someone who might remember
the girl she had been
and could quench her thirst with the waters of oblivion.
And the current swept over tranquil waters
until womanhood emerged as an evident sign
in the center of the living room, in the bedroom,
in second-hand stores,
she bought a red nightgown with unraveled lace
and holes that tumbled down her chest.
She would walk around the house and spill coffee over herself,
cook another book, full of dumplings poisoned by magic
Here the light trickles in slowly like coffee dripping
On a slip the color of exposed skin.
Here she is trying on another dress, daubing on red lipstick.
She was intoxicated by tough thoughts about writing
but also about the clothes strewn in the streets
and the city clothed her and the city wearied her.
She waited for the night,
for sacred days
and whispering birds.

Sophia

Suddenly a rainbow appeared
and Sophia lifted up her children and shouted:
"What a beautiful day! The sun shines and the rain falls
and in the sky a rainbow glows!"
All morning she stole clothes and gave them to the poor.
This is what Sophia knows how to do.
She herself being a very poor woman.
She steals clothes from charity shops
but can't stand the bounty in her own closet.
She has a conscience. She has a good opinion of herself.
She gives them to women left out in the cold.
She always dreamed of being Robin Hood.
Sophia never wanted to complain
complaints might pollute the pure waters
that plunged into her childhood.
But the fire that shattered her mind,
that fire transfigured within her into a caged owl,
poetry will have no room to become beautiful,
if Sophia does not stop cursing, betrayal will be certain
She dreamed of being Robin Hood,
there was no way she could just be a simple woman.

A Poem for Gali

On Gali's roof the sun blazes.
Naked dolls stand like statues
staring, stunned, into the eyes of unwavering loneliness
and scorning all the man-made plans
that stay still in the heart of divine ridicule.
What an omen it is to listen to the sound of airplanes.
Maybe a white balloon, held by its tail with a loving hand,
will come to Gali too
will let her hover above the trash cans
inhabited by rats hungry for intimacy
like polluted air that holds hope
so that the doll can come to life
and move its hands into an embrace
and the fear dissipates with the dawn
radiant in her shuttered window.

Birthday 2010

1

Today is a birthday and I chose her
I bought her soap and she said:
"Whoever is blessed with good luck is the one who gives the blessing,"
And I blessed her with the scent of green soap
So that she'll know physical love. And she is bound up
In her hardened soul and in her abstaining body.
She lives among the clouds and her hair is gilded
Like the sun. Her breasts lunar,
Her belly long. The body enfolded in its womanhood
Is compelled to chase after the coins that permit her
To live close to the heavens, among the fall clouds,
Beneath the blue awning,
Where a sliver of the sea deceives her
That not far from here Nature breathes
And airplanes threaten to crash
Into her pure-white bed.

2

When her floor is swept away by mud
Ants bite her neck
And she no longer understands either the meaning of it
Or what to chase
When a red bulge blooms on her neck
And a bitter curse on the man who promised
To exterminate the sting.

The masses in the street discomfit her
Like stores filled with everything
She can't afford to buy, to perfume herself with, to sink into,
To forget, she chooses the essence and calls it
Work. She doesn't want to forget.
She doesn't want soap for her abstaining body,
Which at night cut its golden hair in the shower
And focuses its power to forge an un-coined reality
It spread a yoga mat at the foot of the bed
And waited for love.

3

Today is a birthday and I chose her.
I gave her soap and said:
"Love is the desire to shelter the beloved."
And she answered: "Only if it's bad
Is there a need to set him free."
And then she went silent and remembered she had been freed
And went to look for someone who would want her,
But she hasn't yet met that man.
Refusing to forget, she will laugh with a trembling heart.
That's just her life,
The roof, the blue awning, the heavens,
The clouds and the sea.
She puts armor on her shoulders
Wears black pants and an undershirt.
Sometimes, facing the mirror, she'll remember her body
The lunar breasts, the long belly,
The pure-white of her empty bed.

Sasha

Sasha lives near lions and tigers
Between sea and mountain, between "two are better than one"
And one. Raven-haired Sasha, where have you gone?
Between the road and the air, between the fields and the city square
Where do your wings swell at night?
Where do they sprout from your back and flutter?

Sasha makes love with anyone who wants it
She loves it here and now
She loves it on the fly.
She leads widows by the hand through darkened streets,
She rocks orphans to sleep,
Sasha loves them all.

Sasha, do you still fear Friday nights?
When the sky douses all the words, do you
Still sit alone, light a cigarette and blow smoke
Into your white room?

Sasha, black of gaze, offers her body
At the speed of sound, surrendering to the heart.
She refuses to stop and think
She trusts that if it must happen, it will.

Marianne Faithfull

Late at night I opened the front door
of the building. I wanted to eat some tomatoes. I was hungry
and didn't know where to get tomatoes. The photos on the walls
looked like tomatoes and I crossed through the gate and slipped into a photo
of Marianne Faithfull and her cheeks looked like two tomatoes
and her eyes like two founts of white heroin, and I wanted
to dive into her eyes and learn the philosophy
of those who survived the white death.
This time Marianne stayed silent and did not sing,
she just dipped into warm water
and her white legs traced upwards in purple circles of dreams
and I wanted to get into the tub filled with domination
and tear away with my nails the distance between us
and very gently whisper to her that Lucy Jordan should not have
jumped from the roof, even though her family did not see
how much her body had been depleted of life.
And to pour her a beer and rest my head on her shoulder.

.

Lucy Jordan

All this Nothing killed her
Dumped the body on the mattress
The tube of her body was squeezed
Like toothpaste at the hands of a baby
And her breath became one
With her closed eyes.
All this Nothing was heaped with life
And accessories for old age.
All this nothing was too much for her
She sighed almost ceaselessly.
All this nothing was full of flesh
And pure kisses.
The stabbing hardship had softened her face
And dulled each sting.
All this nothing was full of filth
And of hatred paralyzed
By an excess of love.

The Scarf

For David Mor

You gave me her scarf to remind me of the ephemeral.
So I won't forget that there was a woman you loved.
Every week you showed me her photo,
She in a black bathing suit, leaning on a tree trunk
A radiant beam stroking her face. She's happy.
It's clear from her look that she had conquered a world for herself
That all is well with her and that her life will be wonderful.
She's married to a painter, has two girls
And he gave her a scarf white as cream
That can be smeared on shoulders
Draped in round loops.
It carries a nice musty smell, a fragrance distilled from the ephemeral.
I wrap it around my shoulders and remember
That you loved her.

Anima

For Ziva Dayan, mother of Yehonatan and Ariel

A woman falls to earth
Without Anima
Or spirit
Anonymous to the weeds
Ants call her by name
Sand encases her face
Roots sprout from her tongue.
A woman is interred in the pit
And her shell is emptied of spirit
Diapered in white like the day she was born
Her legs will not lift her to walk
But the Anima
Frees itself through her nose
And flutters like a kite held by her child
All the way back home.

*

What have you left behind?
Five empty rooms
And the cold spirit of an air-conditioner. August
Slays everything on the ocher earth
Beneath which you are hidden
In the final darkness.
There's a leak in your house. A plumber was called
He bore two holes in the ground, the source of the leak
Went undiscovered. He made a call and shouted over the phone:
The water is flowing, the meter is running, and there's no sign of water.
He promised that someone else would come in twenty-four hours.
Joshua stood in the corner of the garden and bowed his head.
His white beard is a week and a half old.
The scent of your feet lingers still
In the green shoe closet, trapped in your pink sandals.
An orphaned bottle of nail-polish remover in the shower.
Your jewelry has been collected into a tin can and hidden away in the closet.

The Hall
of Ghosts

No Room

Now I'll let the madness out. I'll be its punching bag. I'll be a hot delivery of distress. I'll howl the white nights away. Night abrades against the day. Day devours night. Sobbing. Distress. Innumerable murmurs. Forgetting to put out medicine. Forgetting to put out medicine. Innumerable murmurs. Ear infection. Coughing. Medicine doesn't arrive. Winter. I should study medicine. Should put out the medicine. Should clean the nose. Help. White night. Delirium upon dream upon delirium. To give medicine.

Not to think about myself. I have no room now. Not to think about myself. Not to think about myself. To think only about her. If I think about myself I won't give her medicine.

I was once a girl who sat and wrote in a blank notebook. I pretended for you. I pretended for your camera. I held the pen and penned nothing. I just held it and waited for you to take the picture. You were a father who strove for motherhood. You were a fatherly mother, a motherly father, unsoft but affectionate. And you gave everything, to your last breath, and you were sick and I did not find you a cure. And I was sick and I came to your bed and you told me you have no medicine. And no answer. And I didn't know what to do. And I didn't know where to turn. And you were sick and saw split-tongued Death poised before you waiting. And you didn't want to run into his open arms. And I'm on my knees next to your bed. You had no more breath.

I took murderous medicines. I was drugged as you lay dying. The more you died the more I drugged up. You were by then something else. And there was neither cure nor answer. Except the Red Angel waiting for your death. He had a long, persevering spirit. He had black stifling wings. Full of patience, lusting for your death. And you were ascending ladders of the spirit and your breathing became shallower. And you were waiting for your death. Outside the window, a scorching light. A light as clear as a new sheet, winding around your eyes. And I didn't know where to turn. And I came to you at night and pleaded for an answer. And I came to you and feared my life and, what is more, feared your death. And you had no answer. And I had no medicine.

Once I poised the pen on a blank notebook. I sat on the edge of the seat, my feet in white socks. I wore blue jeans and a striped velvet shirt. I kept a straight face and held my breath. I waited for the photograph. You stood at the end of the hall, outside the door. On the shelf sat a brown teddy-bear with outstretched arms and a red dress. I pretended to write because I knew that was the cure.

Your eyes were contented and the camera captured a slice of the 1980s. Afterwards I went back to the living room to watch TV, leaving the notebook on the empty table. Your eldest daughter's table. The daughter you loved. And for a moment I impersonated your first-born. For a brief moment I was your beloved daughter, focused on pretend writing. You caught my serious glance and I was the one you loved. Twenty years later, I wrote you a real book. I put your photograph on the cover. You sat on the white snow and became an inspiration for orphans. An orphan like you could have no other fate. I wrote you poems. I was your loving daughter and I knew that you loved me.

A Poem for Annette, Woman of Freedom

There's a white void here that I don't want to leave
A pink eye bleeding a blue pupil
A heart spilling from the hands
A round black eye.
There's a white void here that I don't want to leave
And Annette, woman of freedom, treads lightly.
There's a white room here that I don't want to leave
High-ceilinged, grey wood tiles,
Annette gazes at the heart spilling from the hands
And a great laughter on the face of one holding the heart.

Annette understood that freedom is the real joy
So during a time of love she feels trapped
As if there were no room for her to walk upright,
To parade proudly through the streets of Jaffa,
Her golden hair blending with the sun.
Sometimes she is attacked by thoughts of tough
Love. Together we strolled through the gallery and saw sky,
The cerulean horizon, and white clouds coiling over the sea.
Now Yefet Street is backed up in the direction of Bat-Yam
And Annette has vanished into the sun.

Imagine

Imagine you walk down the street, you cross the road
and meet a beautiful man. He kisses you on the cheek
and you laugh in his arms, right there in the middle of the street.
"It's classic," he whispers in your ear, and you continue to walk
in the opposite direction, aimlessly wandering the streets,
swirling around the nothingness, seeking Jerusalem
under all its heavy cosmetics of hats and gloves,
perfumes, spices, socks, toys, expensive shoes,
overpriced dresses, people begging for coins.

Gradually the temperature falls, your hands freeze.
Heavy tears trail down your cheeks.
You are lost even to yourself.

Imagine that instead of continuing to walk, you turn
toward that beautiful man and ask where he is headed.
Perhaps to a café
and perhaps he would have made you laugh
for the remainder of the day.

Poetry

For Noam Glazer-Eitan

Poetry is a bright young woman of twenty-five
Who once lived by herself in Paris and came back depressed.
Her lover writes her poems, which she hangs on the walls of her room.
In the afternoons she sees a psychiatrist and swallows pills,
The pleasantness of her transparent skin failing to shield her body.
She wears a red dress and blue shoes
Sips arak with a straw.
Before bed she puts in a mouth-guard to stop her from grinding her teeth.
Her auburn hair touches her shoulders and she
Whispers a story about a girl in a coma
Whom she does not wish to stir.

Sylvia Plath

The electricity bills and the little girl's cry ate away at you.
The pen that ran out of ink, the typewriter ribbon that dried up
Like the time to write and the strength to face a blank page.
Sorrow sank its roots into the swamp where once Narcissus fell in love.
And one winter everything turned against you, and there was no more light,
Nor a man who would lift your chin up,
The money in the bank account evaporated
Like the mist that rose from the sewers that February.
Snow swathed the windows of your house. Your eldest daughter,
Frieda, no longer took the breast.
What a terrible thing you have done, Sylvia.

Tami

She hasn't yet wiped
the chocolate from her lips
and already she's contemplating a bullet
to the head. For it's impossible to remain
chained to the confectioner's
so Tami goes out to play with
witches. They tell her
that there is freedom, but only for others,
because Tami is always pregnant,
but she likes to smoke. She buys
chocolate and cigarettes, she wants
to be somewhere else. But
the confectioner's smells like
aftershave and Tami likes
to play. Her head is full
full and her heart roars: Help!
I have milk in my veins.
Milk instead of blood. I'm turning into
a wild animal and when I think
about it I fume and then
the aftershave evaporates and goes off
to play with another Tami.

Snow White

Everyone loves Snow White
because of her black hair, blue
eyes, and abandonment. Because her mother
threw her out of the house
her beauty is at risk
and might one day
fade. Because her heart is liable
to get ripped out. Everyone loves
Snow White because of the black
and blue. But Snow White
does not love Snow White
she loves anything
that might erase the black
and blue. Anything that might
make her a grave. Her white
gloves are pinned to the wall
in the prince's palace, a balding man
with a merciful heart which often
hardens. No, she cannot
escape. She is convinced that the prince
is everything she aspired to in the forest
before she met the dwarves
who clambered over her pure-white body,
rose up, lifted, and licked her,
but the dwarves live in a commune
and deep down Snow White is
rather traditional.

The Wolf-Boy

He wanted to see what was in me.
Gold, maybe? Maybe the wolf-boy came to me
to huff and to puff at all that he lacked. His arms
orphaned by a mother who never was. And so too with me,
through my window
I waited for him and he came so I placed on his head a bandage
sterilized of pain.
And this wolf-boy who huffed and puffed my breath
who huffed in surrendering to what he lacked, his forehead
always bore the bandage of his fear.
I play music and lend him something absolute and total
I lend it in exchange for his love.

*

You gorge yourself on men, gorge yourself on men
vile, despicable, worthless.
Everyone thinks you're damaged,
that something in you is cracked and lost.

That you read the wrong
books, that you're too
spectral and afraid.

You gorge yourself on men, gorge yourself on men
You exterminate city mice
A heap of cat hair in your room
Your underwear white with fur.

You could not fulfill every wish
but at night you found the blue bird
and had the time to strum its feathers.

*

I'll be better now
I'll be as though at the end of a night of love. I'll kiss strangers.
The man helped me keep death at bay
I'll be better.
I'll limit myself and will no longer crave drugs.
I'm screwing a man
who knows nothing about me
bedding someone who does not
know my last name.
But in the evening, on the boulevard, for a brief moment
my fingernails brushed across his arm.
Only for the sake of life did I come to him
Complex, like an unfinished poem,
and he's in no rush and moves over me unhurriedly,
unpins my hair pin by pin,
scatters the locks of my hair over the pillow,
crowns my head in his arms like one who has found a treasure.
I sensed that his body was far from expert in this kind of love
because another woman had engraved her place in his arms.
But even in her absence she was present
and I was just a guest,
not invited to engrave my place in his flesh. I closed my eyes
encircled his nape with my hand,
thrilled to the heat of his gestures,
until my bones burst. And at the same time
prevented from believing in his love.
It's a mere mirage,
the faintest facsimile of love.

Gabriel

Gabriel has encircling transparent arms,
a long glistening belly.
His mother tongue: French.
At the upward reaches of his mouth his language is foreign
and below: Hebrew.
He wishes to devour his own heart.
His brain cells are peeling, a strange alliance on his lips.
He falls on the lawn behind the grey building
and deepens his awareness of the grass. Ants make him panic.
Butterflies awaken. The red roof burns.
He shouts. Like the appearance of movement experienced as sound,
his lower lip bitten under his upper teeth.
He masturbates in silence. Semen-sedative is released through his body.
He bites his lip and is becalmed.

Constancy

There was always a poem at the end of the notebook
that brought him back to his place
but to write it
he had to forget his name
the appearance of his face in the mirror.
He abandoned everything inscribed on his fate
like a pillow that had shed its feathers.
He leaped through his window onto the poem
and ambushed himself in the secrecy of night
that arises with the day
and became a winged cat
an owl with sharpened teeth
and tore at his bowels to give birth to his words
just because it was free
and he had no money.

Creation

Above the valley is a child, his mouth in the flowerbed
gathering rain from the sea
when the wind yields, the body of summer is calmer
and the sea reaches the level of the swamp
determined to free itself from seaweed
from the scum-covered black ravines
wave-spray carries seeds
into the verdant valley, rising to disturb
a dream that sprinkles onto a delicate-bodied boy,
he and his mouth in the flowerbed
and a worm stretching from his lips like drool
he gathers up compounded leaves
when his spirit yields and the sting dies down
to pollinate the ever-spreading wild grain
the familiar reddish thorns
the pink-veined rain-flowers
pollinate a pale redness in his soul
and the pile of the leaves becomes still
the familiar pollinates a light redness
flaming from a warm subterranean tapestry
on the face and the legs,
a rose.

The Guitarist

For Ophir Lokay

This night will strike him with vertigo
guitar notes twirling on the walls
he will no longer play her for the sake of the song
but in order to live.
He strums her in the heart of the theater,
as a grey light cathedrals a smoky chamber around them.
On Allenby, Breslov hasids burst out in a light-struck dance.
In the market square a naked diva teases a drunk messiah,
and at the stage's edge, unclouded by words,
his hands move over her breadth
his head bends towards her yellow neck
the light goes out.
Twirling around his touch
she spills secrets from the room.
Tonight Ophir's tones flicker on the walls
he stands in his chamber
at the edge of the stage
and dances.

A Poem for a Literary Editor

I'd just been practicing yoga
after a long period being short of breath
and right then a literary editor called me
and I should have stayed on my back
taking deep breaths
but instead of staying on my back
I got up to toy with a pink rubber ball
and bounced it on the floor
my legs apart, I'm a girl,
sitting on the edge of a yoga mat
bouncing a pink ball.
And my entire future seemed to hang
on this phone call
and heavy clouds linger outside
and I have no money in my pocket
and I share all of the news
and reveal all the secrets,
cut off from the world.
I told him that he can take me
that I am his and that if he wants I'll have no other editor.
I gave in too quickly
even before he could catch me
he threw me back to myself.

A February Night

For Ilan Berkovich

How can oblivion infiltrate the flood of words
notched into the base of cold trees
and frozen into the awareness. They will not impart water.
Startled cats raise their heads
they wish to remain hushed
but your ear was there
strong and silent, steadfast
and so lucid that it was possible to draw with it and tell.
The words soothed me as much as aspirin
would a dead woman,
and no one was there
other than you.
And I walked by your side to the edge of the street
regretfully, diminishing with each passing step.
When we reached the traffic light
I was five years old
and by the time we crossed
I was no longer.

Poison Poetic

For Amichai Shalev

To write under the inspiration of antibiotics
an overdose of Moxypen Forte 500 and Acamol
to write from the lowest place
in time
where the eyes are suspended in the air
searching through them for darkened windows.
To write crooked lines about disrupting life, desperate to live
through the mist the eyes close
a warming sun shines through the window although it's almost January
fingernails clean of the dose of Moxypen 500, ringing resounding resonance
it's impossible to swallow the saliva but there's a strong urge to spit it out
to spit spit on drivers' indifference to birds
and people's indifference to poetry.
To write under the inspiration of an overdose, five red pills
ten white and another ten, nearly a full packet of chocolate
and a throat sobbing in agony. It's impossible to swallow
it, impossible to open the blinds onto regular
realms. Now it's time for the chin to sink into the left arm.
There's a rumor running around that everything will be over
in forty-eight hours.
At the poison center the hotline is busy.
I haven't been loved for a year now.
These are my last words and in a little while
I'll celebrate liberation from my body.

Emily and Emmanuel

The closed room clutches naked bodies, refuses to reveal the secrets of limbs
Emily is erased by each raven that squawks on the hotel roof,
Emmanuel sinks into her flesh, his face disappearing.
She a girl and he a man, she doesn't speak English and he
is a poet in three languages.
Emily fell into Emmanuel's ocean and the sealed rooms do not
expose either body-theft or penetration.
Emily swims among divine words, strides hand in hand toward
another Emily who will see her reflection in the mirror and won't understand.
The telephone is off. No one comes or goes.
The other Emily walks in the street, her hand holding Emmanuel's,
learning to swim, like a red fish, amid other words.
She reads poetry, a flock of ravens squawks overhead.
All the ravens of Ukraine spread their wings,
rest on the tops of trees that shed yellowed brittle leaves.
A flock of ravens squawks:
"Lovers, too, must use their vision, must be reminded of their lonely
existences, their receding bones and hands."
But Emmanuel doesn't abandon Emily even for a minute.
Emmanuel drinks in her soul and Emily listens to every word,
walks hand in hand
in the darkened Czernowitz streets, night falls and Paris is far away.
The ravens offer their beds in the fir-tree tops
and Emily dips into the bath, her thighs scorched, infected by all her childlike
strength. Emmanuel doesn't loosen his grip on her hand,
not even for an hour, he wants
to know her interior, to use all the Emilyan sun.
The ravens take hold of Emily's hair and hoist her skyward,
the ravens peck their beaks into Emmanuel's arms and lift him skyward,
Emmanuel and Emily left their bodily scent in the room and flew
back to Kiev and from there on ravens' wings to Paris.
Emily will not know who awaits her in the mirror. Emmanuel might get word
that their time is up. Emily will be left with memories of someone
who dreamt of a life beside a poet

and long conversations into the night
which trundles along the tracks.

That Crazy Night

Do you remember that crazy night?
When I forced the whole room to listen to my poems
and then I came to you and kissed you on the lips?
You didn't know who I was. In other words, we hadn't met. I just saw you
standing on the side talking with some professor,
dark circles under your eyes.
The moment I remember those dark circles
I get the urge to smoke something really strong.
Maybe because that night I rolled cigarettes for everyone in the room.
Afterwards you took me home. Even though I didn't want to go.
You listened to my poems on the radio in your car
and when we arrived I discovered you were a vampire.
You sat on the couch and seemed so sad.
You had sunk into the depths of some hole within you.
And I did not want to come to you.
I told you I had someone else.
To this day I regret having said that.
I regret not having hugged you, not having kissed you.
Not having plunged into your abyss, filling it with my whole being.
With my poems. With everything you feared to look at
for more than a single night.

To: The Salvation of Mary

Greetings

RE: Memorandum: Spider

On 24.4.2004, a black spider spun a long-threaded web and with an iron finger rolled you with its fist into a Golem.
You received a debt in the amount of your life for: "Relief. Relief" which buzzed and used up all its strength for its repulsive groaning.
How awful is that moment in which he acts for his life and your death.
Unfortunately, you have yet to repay your debt to the spider.
Immediately upon your arrival he lowered your spirit to nothing, to a television set; it pressed the button and turned up your volume.
You take no offense for its sake, a woman like you doesn't demand a bill.
A lonely woman like you hasn't the strength to refuse.
From now on you are kindly requested to leave without asking permission, even when the spider stands in your way, and when you flee, grasp the door handle more firmly. Look carefully, maybe you'll find the key. And if the spider chafes against your dress like a dog and barks "relief, relief," and if it turns you over and the handle presses into your belly and your fingernails furrow the wall plaster, do not wail in lament and do not cry out to the gods.

You are kindly requested to pay the bill within seven days from receipt of this letter. You may pay in one of three ways:
— Submit a complaint by presenting this stub at any police station.
— Arrange a mercenary payment by calling 1-666-666-666.
— Visit one of our nearby branches and rent a gun.

For your information, after payment has been issued, according to the legal statute pertaining to rape victims (1975) you are eligible to receive compensation from the insurance agency representing the man who did to you what he did.

If the debt has been paid, please consider the present letter null and void. If, however, the debt has not been regularised as specified above, our office will be forced to take any means at its disposal to collect the compensation due to you according to the law and/or an agreement reached between the parties.

"How much does your courage cost?" he asked, as I pointed the pistol at him.
"What price do you put on it?" I asked.
"Courage happens to be in demand these days," he laughed.
"And is there a demand for decency?"
"Yes, but only if you're prepared to sell that too," he replied.
And then

With regards and blessings,
I Shot Twice.

Desdemona

Desdemona

1

My mother's eyes went blind.
I am transported by the fragrance of her blindness,
By her love-making body,
I am battered between cold walls.

Like a candlelight halo on mountaintops
I float on a sea of pus as white
as her eyes, the last I saw.
I was always the daughter of others.

Now I am blinded like her
I wear the stones of buildings
whose greyness conquered me.

Now the outrageous place towers high,
The chill blows in from every side
I call my eyes to come back.

2

I call my eyes to come back to you
and you come and reveal yourself in the night,
A chilled woman rises from a biting pillow
You come in close and sink your teeth in

My spurting blood rouges your lips
from which the snow descends, bitter.
I pull my hand to span your hair.
Look at me, I was one of your daughters.

O, how a burnt childhood smells,
my hair is singed by longings,
Smolders with ashen shampoo.

Extinguish the plague incense now
Passion rips my pillow to shreds
Plant on my mouth a toxic mother's kiss.

3

Plant on my mouth a toxic mother's kiss
Even the moon envies you
when you depart to your man
Its shine haloes like a lampshade above your head.

Your image hastens to chase my two eyes
though they are closed in unremitting darkness.
And how can I drop this dream?
Cruel orphanhood grits my teeth.

All trust has forever faded, slain.
More than once you were a hidden mirror for me
a secret burnished vision.

But you weren't there to shield me,
Your image leaps now from my eyes.
The healing of your wound wounded me.

4

The healing of your wound wounded me
So I turn toward another life
I flee to the hills
where I will not be yours.

The rage gathers in you from accumulations
of worthlessness and inferiority
From me you demand independence
but you display only impotence.

You haven't yet shattered the myth
The one that binds you to your family.
Do you demand independence from yourself?

Do you still love without hesitation?
It is enough for you to be his wife.
You are in love with his love.

5

You are in love with his love
So I throw myself on blind
chance. And I imagine another fate,
its strangeness only to my benefit.

I will come to him and ask for refuge,
I will head north toward the mountain
where the strange man awaits me,
who would take and watch over all that is within me.

And an answer there is none, nor any word
except ruins within my belly,
flooded with a dragon tongue's spittle.

He turns on his side and refuses
to admit that I have encountered love
on a night meant only for a funeral.

6

On a night meant only for a funeral,
Jupiter is striped and striated.
My best years are not taking off,
Othello fell asleep without a good word.

At first only the cigarettes suffocated me.
Men who love love die slowly.
But women who love love
die quickly, on a bed of curses.

Above all I hate causeless hatred.
A thorn as long as a tongue
stabs into my eye until the spray fails.

Above the envy of death I bend
the thrusting thorn into the pupil's depths.
My blood waters the flowerpot on the balcony.

7

My blood waters the flowerpot on the balcony
and a clinic door opens. A suffocated
throat is thrown out with a fury
that will not find a reconciling eye.

So what if I'm like that. Hysterical.
As it is I can't cry
As it is this intensifies
into a silent, mute, suppressed pain.

And no, I still don't know
what I have there in my belly. "If
you wait nine months

it will pass," said the doctor of knowledge.
But this is a concealed thing impossible to see
outside the screen that you alone light up.

8

Outside the screen that you alone light up
with the device sheathed with a rubber
when all I asked for was a cutter.
After all, you always appear and cut up

a woman's body. Whether you hear
her pleas, or not. Until she ceases to move
Until her belly resembles the wound of Sodom
O, then you'll turn bowing and cheering

to the dream of a woman who has not yet been born.
Never again will I intone a good girl's voice
I will release the demons by choice.

My eyes return lit up.
From amongst the desolation I will yet give birth,
and from the rib will draw forth love.

Someone Else

Someone else would have stopped
Others stopped and many did not
stop. Something like this is impossible
to stop. The street is crowded with men who stopped
And I in my room yearn and do not stop.
It is impossible to lean on it
Impossible to buy jam with it
But it drizzles honey and air
It smells like home and music
It has what is needful
Everywhere a hole is filled
Any open space receives a sign
A word and a silence.
Anyone who stopped will say stop
Anyone who stopped will say that it's impossible
To lean on it.

9 781848 614772